BE · AN · EXPERT

WEATHER
FORECASTER

Barbara Taylor-Cork

SHOOTING STAR PRESS

This edition produced
in *1995* for
Shooting Star Press Inc
230 Fifth Avenue
Suite 1212
New York NY 10001

Design David West
Children's Book Design
Designer Flick Killerby
Editor Jen Green
Consultant Martin Weitz
Illustrator Creative Hands
and Aziz Khan
Picture Researcher Emma
Krikler

Designed and produced by
NW Books Ltd
28 Percy Street
London W1P 0LD

First published in
the United States in 1992
Gloucester Press Inc.
95 Madison Avenue
New York, NY 10016

ISBN: 1-57335-330-2

Printed in Belgium

Photocredits
Page 4 top: The Hutchinson Library;
page 4 bottom: Planet Earth
Pictures; page 6 and 12: Eye
Ubiquitous; page 14: Paul
Nightingale; pages 16 and 22:
Robert Harding Picture Library;
page 28: Frank Spooner Pictures.

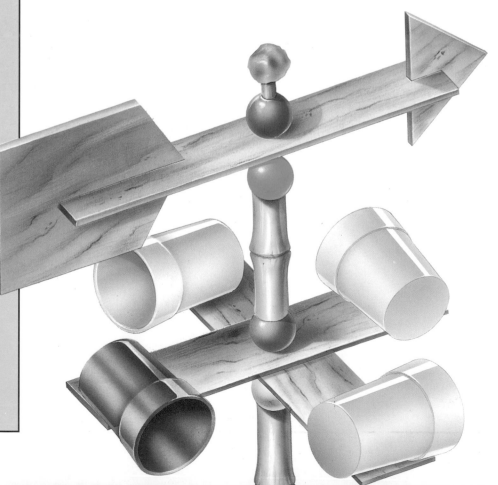

INTRODUCTION

The weather is the state of the air at a particular place and time – how warm or cold it is, how wet or dry, how cloudy the sky is, and how strongly the wind blows. The weather affects our lives every day, from the clothes we wear and the food we eat, to where we live and how we travel.

This book is a practical guide to understanding climate – the usual pattern of weather in a particular area – and to recording and forecasting the weather. With the help of practical projects, it explains how weather is produced. A variety of weather features are described, including clouds, air pressure, and winds. This book explores how pollution of the environment has affected climate. Weather experts use computer technology and data from stations and satellites all over the world to predict the weather. With the aid of this book you can make your own weather-recording equipment. By carefully monitoring weather conditions, you can begin to predict when change is due, and become an expert weather forecaster.

CONTENTS

OUR PLANET
4
DAYS AND SEASONS
6
AIR PRESSURE
12
WHERE THE WIND BLOWS
16
WATER IN THE AIR
20
POLLUTION AND CLIMATE CHANGE
28
MAKING A WEATHER STATION
30
GLOSSARY AND INDEX
32

OUR PLANET

Without the sun, there would be no weather on our planet. Heat from the sun warms the air above the earth. But because the earth has a curved surface, different parts of it receive different amounts of heat. The sun's rays travel to our planet in straight parallel lines. They strike it most directly at the equator around the middle of the earth, so countries there (such as Cameroon in Africa, below) have a hot climate. The rays strike the north and south poles at the top and bottom of the earth least directly, making these regions very cold. In between these two extremes, the weather is less severe. Differences in temperature cause air to move from place to place. Moving air, which we call the wind, carries warmth and coolness around the world, producing all the kinds of weather we know.

Near the poles, the sun's rays have to travel a great distance through the atmosphere. The rays strike the poles at an indirect angle, so they are spread out and have to heat a wider area, losing even more of their heating power. This causes very cold conditions in Arctic regions (above right).

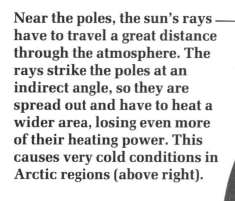

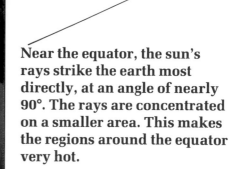

Near the equator, the sun's rays strike the earth most directly, at an angle of nearly 90°. The rays are concentrated on a smaller area. This makes the regions around the equator very hot.

THE ATMOSPHERE

Our planet is surrounded by a protective shield of gases called the atmosphere. More than three-quarters of the atmosphere is nitrogen and most of the rest is oxygen. Less than one percent of it is made up of carbon dioxide and water vapor.

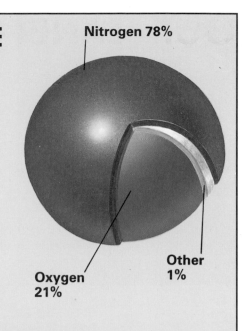

Nitrogen 78%

Oxygen 21%

Other 1%

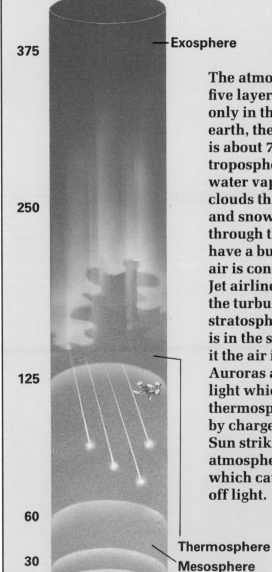

MI

375 — Exosphere

The atmosphere is made up of five layers, but weather occurs only in the layer nearest the earth, the troposphere, which is about 7 miles high. The troposphere contains the most water vapor, which creates the clouds that bring rain, hail, and snow. Aircraft flying through the troposphere may have a bumpy ride because the air is constantly moving there. Jet airliners usually fly above the turbulence in the stratosphere. The ozone layer is in the stratosphere. Beyond it the air is very thin and cold. Auroras are wispy curtains of light which appear in the thermosphere. They are made by charged particles from the Sun striking gases in the atmosphere above the poles, which causes the gases to give off light.

250

125

60

30

6

Thermosphere
Mesosphere
Stratosphere
Ozone layer
Troposphere

The beam of a flashlight on an upright paper is like the sun at the equator. Hold the paper at an angle to see the sun's effect at the poles.

DAYS AND SEASONS

In most parts of the world, the weather changes regularly throughout the year. These changes are called seasons. They are caused by the fact that the earth tilts at an angle of 23.5° on its axis. As the earth moves around the sun, the tilt means that some parts of our planet are closer to or further from the sun. The tilt affects the regions around the poles the most. They experience long hours of daylight in summer, and darkness in winter. The area around the equator is consistently close to the sun, and the lands there are hot all year round. The regions between the poles and the equator become gradually warmer and colder as they tilt toward or away from the sun, giving four seasons: spring, summer, fall, and winter.

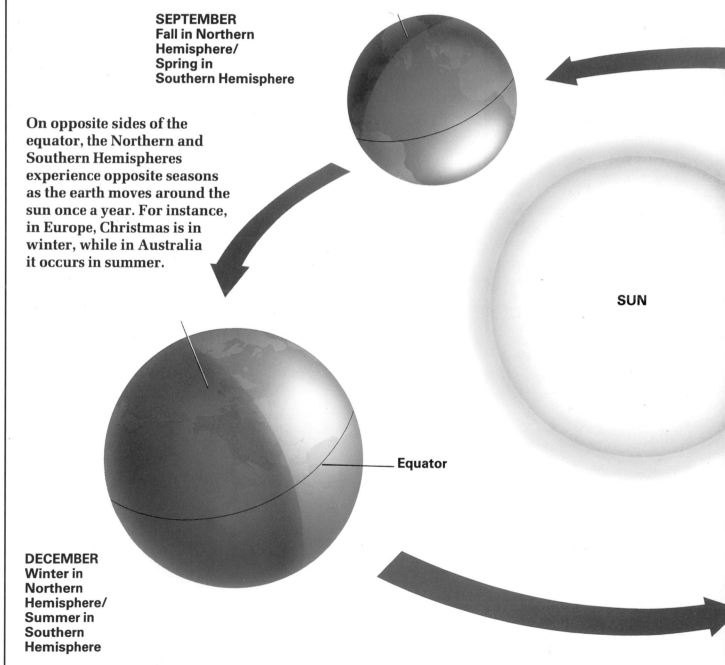

SEPTEMBER
Fall in Northern Hemisphere/
Spring in Southern Hemisphere

On opposite sides of the equator, the Northern and Southern Hemispheres experience opposite seasons as the earth moves around the sun once a year. For instance, in Europe, Christmas is in winter, while in Australia it occurs in summer.

SUN

Equator

DECEMBER
Winter in Northern Hemisphere/
Summer in Southern Hemisphere

THE TILTING EARTH

The earth is tilted on its axis, an imaginary line through the earth between the north and south poles. The tilt always points the same way in space. When the part of the earth where you live is tilted toward the sun, more light and heat reach you. In cold seasons, your country is tilted away from the sun.

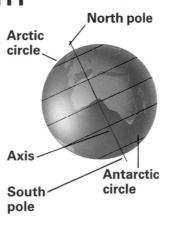

North pole
Arctic circle
Axis
South pole
Antarctic circle

DAY AND NIGHT

Every day, the sun seems to rise in the east and set in the west. But the sun does not really move. Day and night are caused by the earth spinning around on its axis like a top. It spins around once every 24 hours. When the part of the earth where you live is turned to face the sun, it is day. When your part of the earth faces away from the sun, it is night.

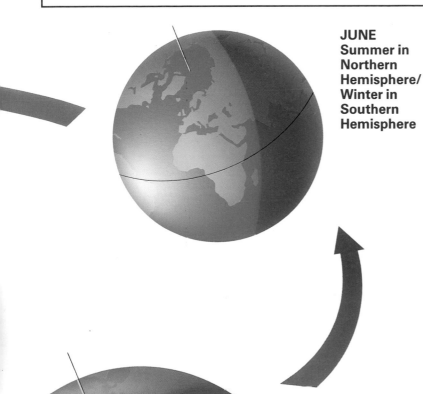

JUNE
Summer in Northern Hemisphere/ Winter in Southern Hemisphere

MARCH
Spring in Northern Hemisphere/ Fall in Southern Hemisphere

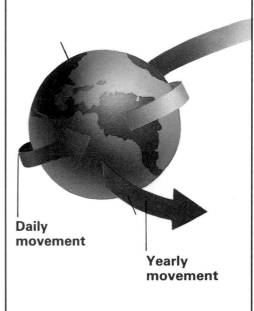

Daily movement

Yearly movement

South pole in sunlight in December

South pole in darkness in June

Because of the tilt of the earth, the sun never sets for six months of the year near the north and south poles. This is why these regions are called the land of the midnight sun. In the summer it is light all the time, and in the winter it is dark all the time.

HOW HOT IS IT?

The temperature in different parts of the world depends on their distance north or south of the equator, which affects the amount and intensity of sunlight they receive. Other factors are also important. Places near the sea usually do not experience great temperature changes, because the sea heats up and cools down more slowly than the land does. Such places are said to have a maritime climate – maritime means "near the sea." The height of the land also affects temperature. The air is cooler the higher up you are.

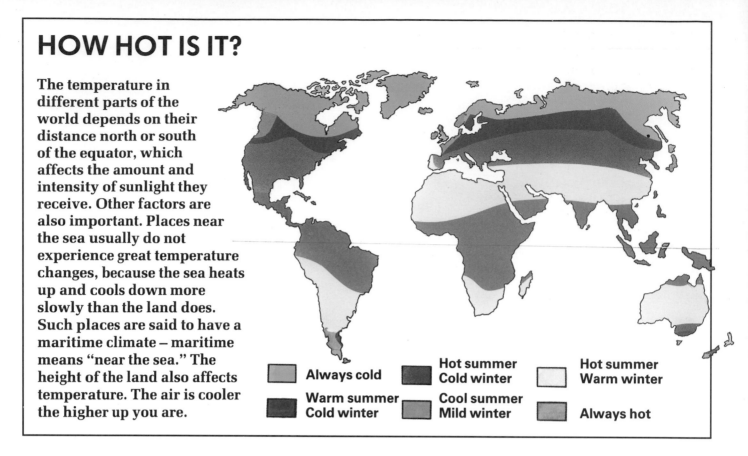

Always cold	Hot summer Cold winter	Hot summer Warm winter
Warm summer Cold winter	Cool summer Mild winter	Always hot

WATCHING THE SEASONS

Keep a record of how the weather changes during the year. Note the length of day and night, how cold it is, and the position of the sun in the sky. Seasons affect the lives of plants and animals. Choose a tree that loses its leaves in the fall. Study the tree each month and note how its appearance changes.

ANIMALS IN WINTER
Animals react to winter in different ways. Some kinds of birds migrate to warmer places in winter. Squirrels survive by eating stores of food. Arctic hares turn white in winter for camouflage against the snow.

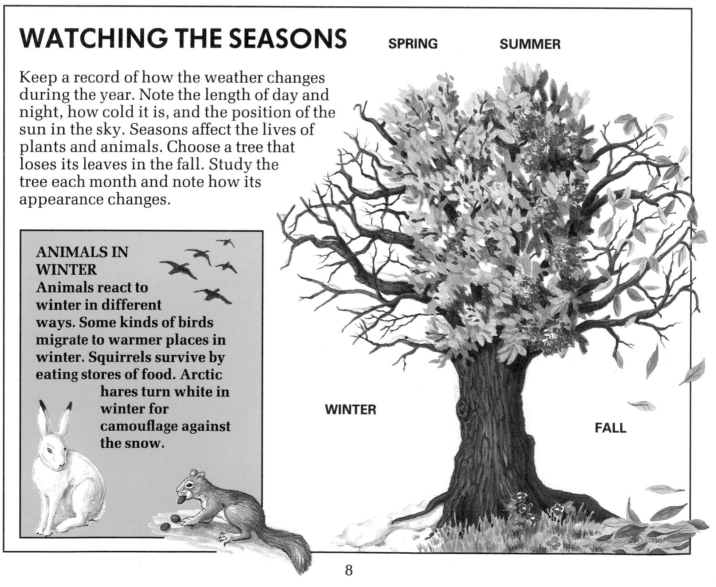

SPRING SUMMER

WINTER

FALL

As the earth turns, the position of any point on it changes in relation to the sun. So shadows cast by objects move throughout the day. Over 3,000 years ago, people invented the sundial, a way of telling the time using shadows from the sun.

Try making a sundial yourself. Mark the center of a square board and ask an adult to help you nail or screw it to a wooden stake. You need a length of strong wire, cut from a coathanger, perhaps. Bend the wire back on itself to make a stand. Attach it securely to the center of the board with hoop tacks or bent nails.

Plant your sundial in the soil on a sunny day. On every hour, check where the shadow falls and mark it on the board. Once you have done this, you will not need a watch to tell the time.

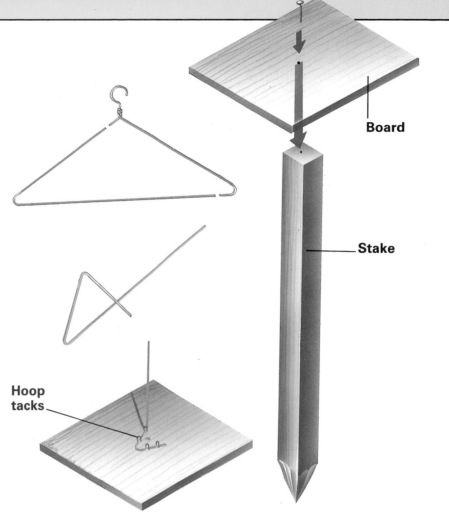

Board

Stake

Hoop tacks

The upright wire which casts a shadow is a gnomon, or shadow marker.

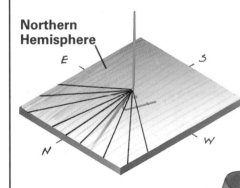

Northern Hemisphere

E   S

N   W

Equator

E   S

N   W

Southern Hemisphere

E   S

N   W

Use a compass to find out the direction of north, south, east, and west. Mark them on your sundial, and position it so that "North" on the dial faces north. If you live in the Northern Hemisphere, the shadow of your gnomon falls in the north. In the Southern Hemisphere, shadows fall to the south. At the equator shadows move, shorten and lengthen slightly each day.

Compass

HOT AND COLD

To understand changes in the weather, it is important to measure air temperature – how hot or cold the air is. Our bodies are not very good at sensing temperature accurately, so we use instruments called thermometers to measure it for us. Many thermometers make use of the way mercury or a liquid such as alcohol expands when it warms up, moving up a thin tube marked with a temperature scale. As the temperature falls, the mercury contracts and falls back down the tube. Maximum and minimum thermometers record the highest and lowest temperatures reached daily.

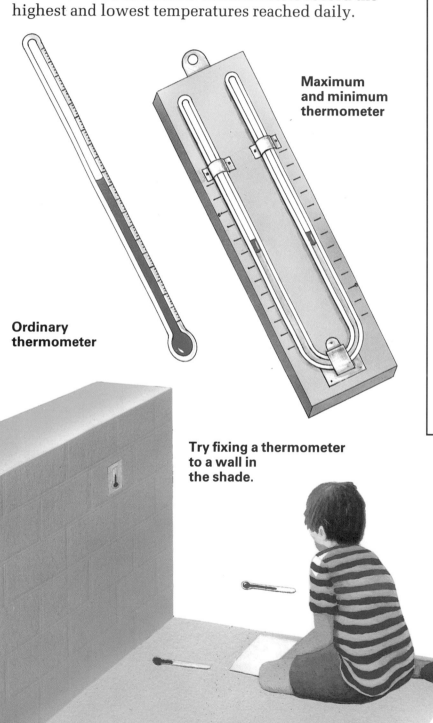

Maximum and minimum thermometer

Ordinary thermometer

Try fixing a thermometer to a wall in the shade.

Air temperature is affected by the season and time of day. To build up a picture of the range in temperature where you live, take recordings from your thermometer at different times of day for one week each month. Draw up a chart for each day on squared paper and fill it in. Try guessing the temperature before you read it off the thermometer. What are the highest and lowest temperatures you record, and at what time of day and year do they occur?

The temperature recorded by your thermometer will vary according to whether you position it in sunlight, in the shade, on the ground, or in the air. Experiment with thermometers in different places and compare the readings they give.

TEMPERATURE SCALES

Temperature is measured in degrees Celsius (°C), or Fahrenheit (°F). To convert °F to °C, subtract 32, multiply by 5 and divide by 9. To convert °C to °F, multiply by 9, divide by 5 and add 32.

WARM AND COOL COLORS

Light and dark colors respond to the sun's rays in different ways. Test this by placing thermometers under light and dark colored paper. Leave them in sunlight or under a lamp for 15-30 minutes. Remove the paper. Which thermometer gives the highest reading? What can you conclude from this about which color it would be best to wear if the weather is hot?

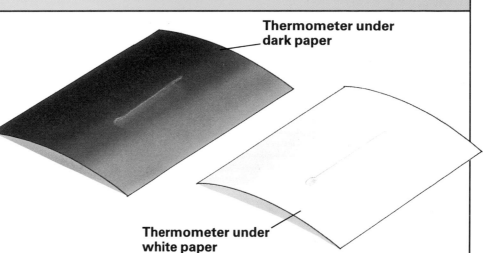

Thermometer under dark paper

Thermometer under white paper

INSULATION

An insulator is a material that prevents the flow of heat. Air is a good insulator; it helps to keep warm things warm and cool things cool. Test this with two thermometers, one wrapped in a towel. Put both in a refrigerator for 30 minutes, then compare readings. The towel traps a layer of air, which does not let cold pass through easily.

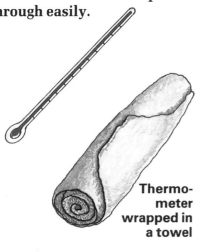

Thermometer wrapped in a towel

LAND AND SEA

Soil

Water

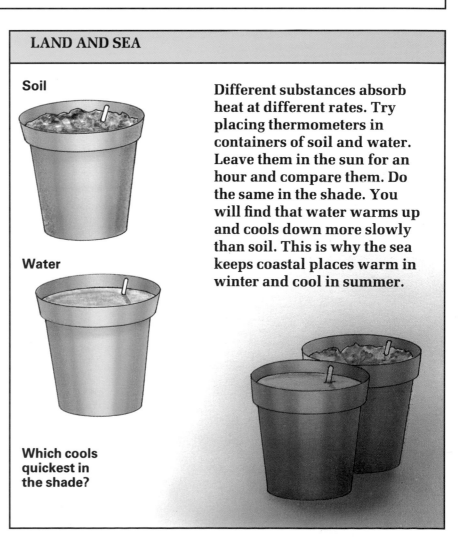

Which cools quickest in the shade?

Different substances absorb heat at different rates. Try placing thermometers in containers of soil and water. Leave them in the sun for an hour and compare them. Do the same in the shade. You will find that water warms up and cools down more slowly than soil. This is why the sea keeps coastal places warm in winter and cool in summer.

AIR PRESSURE

The weight of the air in the atmosphere pressing down on the earth exerts a force called air pressure. We are not usually aware of this force because the air presses equally on us from all directions, and the air inside our bodies presses outward. Cool air is denser or "heavier" than warm air. Warm air is less dense or "lighter," and therefore rises above cool air. When cool air sinks and presses on the ground, it causes an area of high pressure. When warm air rises, it causes a region of low pressure. Air moves from areas of high pressure to areas of low pressure, producing winds.

Air pressure is measured in millibars. Readings over 1010 show high pressure.

Air pressure varies over time from place to place. High pressure is caused by cool air sinking. Low pressure is caused by warm air rising.

HIGH

1040

1032

1016

1000

TWISTING WINDS

As warm air rises and cool air sinks, it is twisted because the earth is spinning around. In the Northern Hemisphere, this causes the winds to spiral anti-clockwise in regions of low pressure, and clockwise in regions of high pressure. In the Southern Hemisphere, the winds spiral in opposite directions.

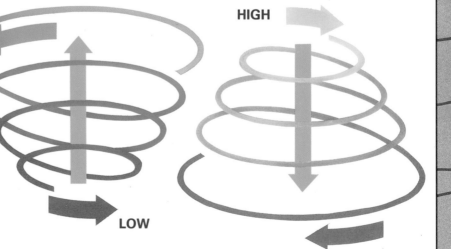

HIGH

LOW

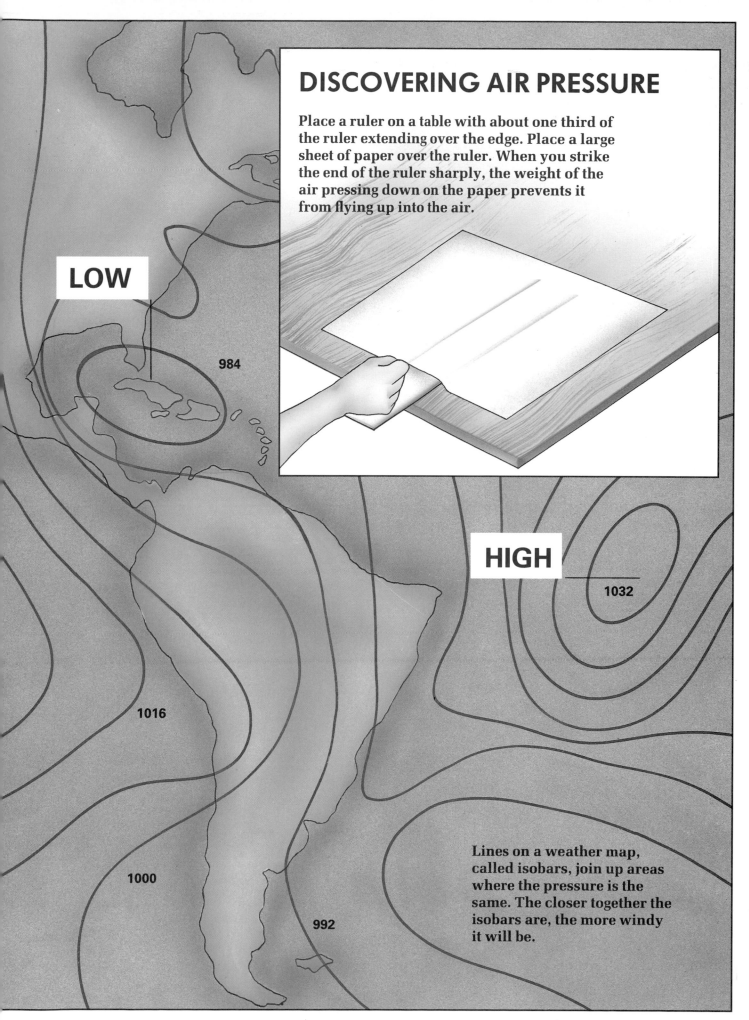

LOW

984

DISCOVERING AIR PRESSURE

Place a ruler on a table with about one third of the ruler extending over the edge. Place a large sheet of paper over the ruler. When you strike the end of the ruler sharply, the weight of the air pressing down on the paper prevents it from flying up into the air.

HIGH

1032

1016

1000

992

Lines on a weather map, called isobars, join up areas where the pressure is the same. The closer together the isobars are, the more windy it will be.

WEIGHING THE AIR

Gravity is the pull that draws objects down toward the center of the earth. It is the force that gives things weight, including air.

Is a balloon heavier or lighter after you blow air into it? Find out by tying a string around the middle of a cane so that the cane balances. Attach an empty balloon to each end of the cane. Then remove one of the balloons and blow air into it. When you attach it to the cane again, this end will dip down, because the air makes the balloon heavier.

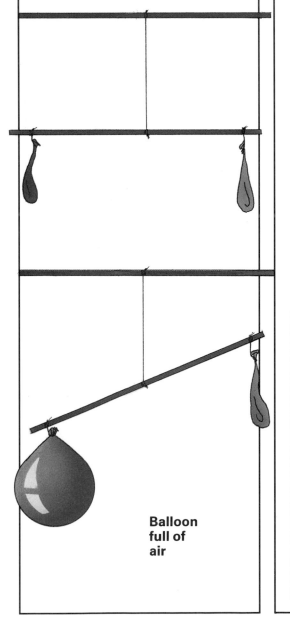

Balloon full of air

Barometers measure air pressure. Air pressure going up means fine, dry weather. Air pressure going down means rain. Water in the air is in the form of a gas, water vapor. Warm air can carry more water vapor than cool air. In areas of low pressure, warm air rises and cools. Some water vapor becomes droplets of water, forming rain clouds. In areas of high pressure, cool air becomes warmer as it sinks down. Warm air holds more water, so it is usually fine.

Barometers are used to predict changes in weather conditions.

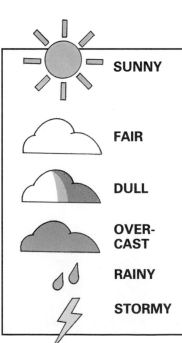

SUNNY

FAIR

DULL

OVER-CAST

RAINY

STORMY

KEEPING A RECORD

Take readings from your barometer each day. Record whether the air pressure is rising or falling. Note the weather and build up a picture of the weather that follows a change in pressure. To make recording easier, invent symbols for different types of weather. When you are practiced at this, you will be able to use your barometer to predict the weather.

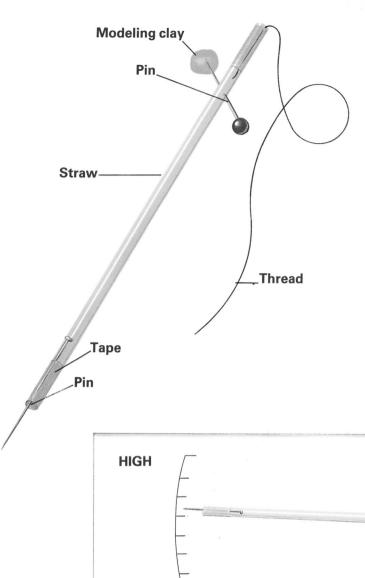

Modeling clay

Pin

Straw

Thread

Tape

Pin

Make a simple barometer by removing the lid of a large empty container. Put plastic wrap over the top and secure it with an elastic band. Tape one end of a cotton thread to the wrap and the other end to a drinking straw. Pierce the straw near the end with a pin. Stand a piece of cardboard behind the container. Pin the straw to the cardboard so that it pivots freely. Put modeling clay on the pin behind the cardboard to secure it.

Tape a pin to the other end of the straw to form a fine pointer. Mark its position on the backing cardboard. Mark the position of the pointer once a day and notice if it is rising or falling. Your marks will form a dial indicating high and low pressure. As the air pressure increases, the pointer will rise. The weather is likely to be dry. When the air pressure falls, the pointer will fall, too. Clouds and rain are likely. If the level stays the same, the weather is not likely to change in the near future.

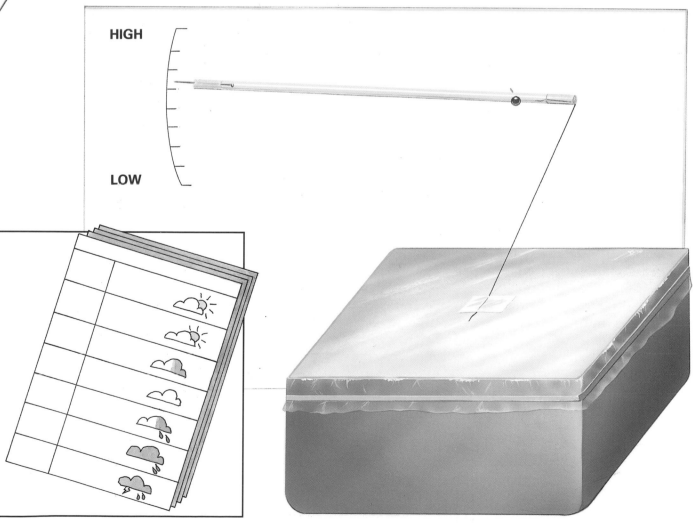

HIGH

LOW

WHERE THE WIND BLOWS

The pattern of the world's winds is controlled by differences in air temperature and pressure over the globe. Warm air rises near the equator and blows toward the poles. Cold air moves in to replace it, blowing in the opposite direction. But because the earth is spinning from west to east, winds do not blow from north to south. Instead they curve to the right north of the equator, and to the left in the south. This is called the Coriolis force. In the middle latitudes – 30-60° north and south of the equator – winds blow mainly from the west (westerlies). Elsewhere they blow mainly from the east.

TRADE WINDS
Sailing ships carrying goods to trade around the world made use of winds that blew steadily toward the equator from the northeast or the southeast. These became known as trade winds.

Equatorial trough

THE DOLDRUMS
The Doldrums are an area of low pressure along the equator where the trade winds meet. Sailing ships avoid this area because the winds are calm or very light, and do not push the ships along.

HURRICANES
Tropical regions sometimes experience violent storms, in which high winds swirl around in a circle. In the Caribbean these are called hurricanes (pictured above). They form over the west Atlantic Ocean where trade winds meet. Weather experts give them names such as "Betsy" or "Claude" to identify them.

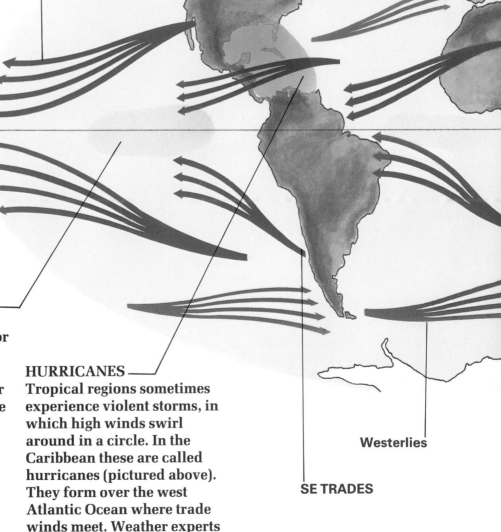

Westerlies

NE TRADES

Westerlies

SE TRADES

TYPHOONS

In the China Seas, tropical storms are known as typhoons. In the Indian Ocean and the seas north of Australia they are called cyclones. They begin as small thunderstorms, but can grow into swirling masses of cloud hundreds of miles across.

NAMING THE WINDS

Many small, local winds influence the weather in different parts of the world. For instance, the mistral is a cold northwesterly wind that funnels down the Rhone Valley in France. The harmattan blows south from the Sahara across West Africa, bringing dust storms and very dry air. In the Mediterranean, the levante wind is an easterly wind which brings mild, moist air to Gibraltar and to the mainland of Spain and Africa. The middle of large continents are the source of many cold winds, such as the pampero, a very cold southwesterly wind which blows across the Pampas grasslands in Argentina, in South America.

1, 2 Norther winds
3 Norte winds
4, 5 Canadian blizzards
6 Ice cap blizzards
7 Buran or Purga winds
8 Föhn winds
9 Bora winds
10 Mistral winds
11 Levante winds
12 Harmattan winds
13 Haboob dust storms
14 Berg winds
15 Shamal winds
16 Seistan winds
17 Karaburan winds
18 Brickfield winds
19 Nor'wester winds
20 Southerly Busters
21 Polar winds
22 Pampero storms

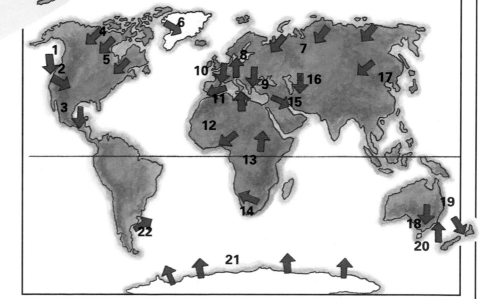

ROARING FORTIES

The Roaring Forties are furious, westerly winds which rage almost constantly in the Southern Hemisphere. They occur at a latitude of 40°.

The wind can be measured with various devices. Weather vanes swing around to show which direction the wind is blowing from. An instrument called an anemometer measures wind speed. Its little cups catch the wind and spin around very fast in a strong breeze. A recording device counts how many times they spin around in a given period.

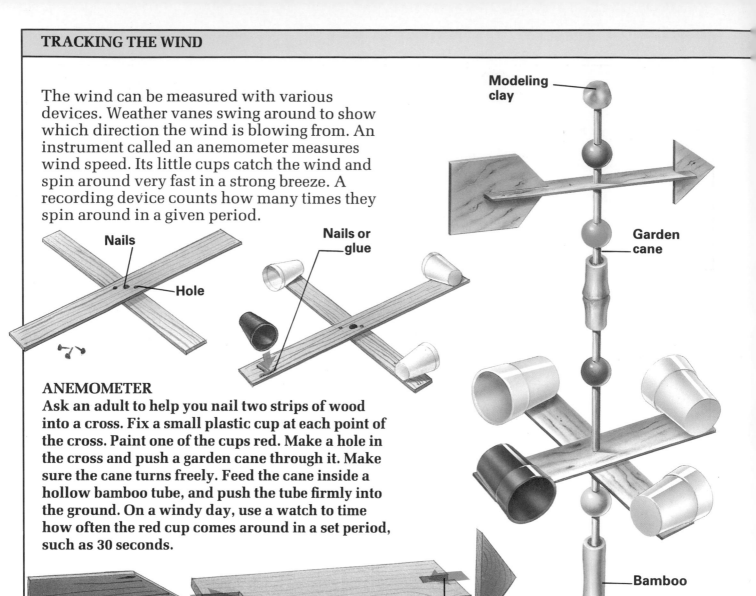

Nails

Hole

Nails or glue

Modeling clay

Garden cane

ANEMOMETER

Ask an adult to help you nail two strips of wood into a cross. Fix a small plastic cup at each point of the cross. Paint one of the cups red. Make a hole in the cross and push a garden cane through it. Make sure the cane turns freely. Feed the cane inside a hollow bamboo tube, and push the tube firmly into the ground. On a windy day, use a watch to time how often the red cup comes around in a set period, such as 30 seconds.

Glue

Bamboo

Use beads and bamboo tubing to keep the wind vane and the anemometer separate.

Push into ground

WIND VANE

Cut slots in a strip of balsa wood. Glue a pointer on one end and a tail on the other end. Make a hole through the middle of the vane and place it above your anemometer, making sure it can move freely.

THE BEAUFORT SCALE

In 1805, Admiral Beaufort invented a scale for measuring winds at sea by describing their effect on ships and waves. His scale was given symbols and adapted for use on land. The same system is still in use today.

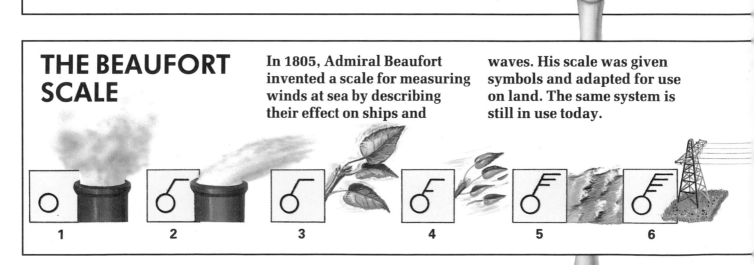

1

2

3

4

5

6

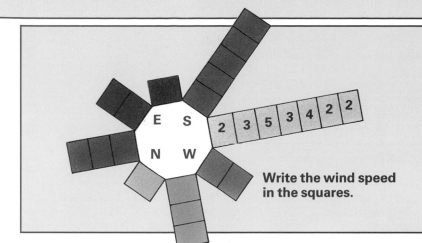

Write the wind speed in the squares.

WIND ROSE

Plot your wind records on a chart called a wind rose. Each day, color in one square that points in the direction the wind is blowing from. Work out the wind speed using the Beaufort scale and your anemometer readings.

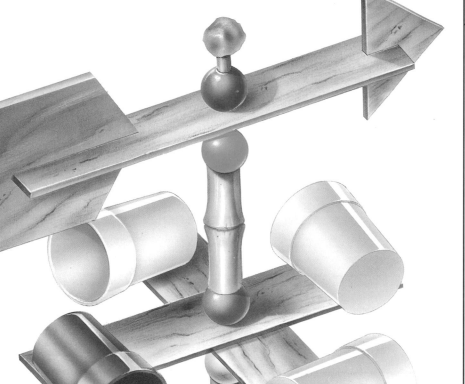

PORTABLE ANEMOMETER

This anemometer will fit on a windowsill. Tape a ping pong ball to a strip of cardboard. Use a protractor to draw a scale on a piece of thick cardboard. Pin the strip to the cardboard and cut a window so you can read the scale.

Angle:	80°	60°	40°	20°
MPH	8	15	21	32

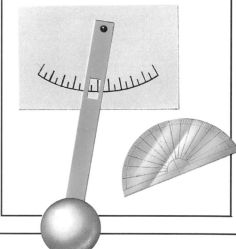

1 Calm – no wind.
2 Smoke drifts.
3 Leaves and twigs move, flags flutter.
4 Small branches move.

5 Crests in water.
6 Wind whistles in electric and telephone wires.
7 Whole trees sway.
8 It becomes difficult to walk.

9 Tiles are blown from roof tops.
10 Trees are uprooted.
11 Widespread damage is caused to buildings.
12 Devastation is caused.

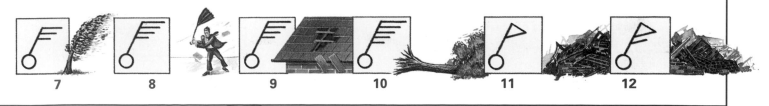

7　　8　　9　　10　　11　　12

WATER IN THE AIR

The air is full of water, but it is usually in the form of an invisible gas called water vapor. As air rises, it cools and some of the water vapor turns into drops of liquid, which gather together to form clouds. This process is called condensation. Air may rise for various reasons. It may rise over mountainous terrain, or when it is heated and made lighter by warm ground. Or it may rise because cold, heavy air pushes under it, forcing it upward. The shape, color, and height of the clouds that result from condensation provide clues to the weather over the next hours or days.

CIRROCUMULUS
High in the atmosphere, water droplets freeze into ice crystals. Cirrocumulus clouds are waves of ice crystals.

FAMILIES OF CLOUDS
There are three main groups of clouds. High-level, wispy clouds are cirrus, from the Latin word meaning "curl of hair." Fluffy clouds are cumulus, meaning "heap." Lowlevel blankets of cloud are stratus, meaning "layer." Clouds have different symbols, shown here. Sometimes cloud types and names are combined.

ALTOCUMULUS
Alto is Latin for "high up." Altocumulus clouds look like cotton balls, and are a sign that unsettled weather is on the way.

THE WATER CYCLE

Water moves up into the sky and back to the ground again in a never-ending cycle. As the sun's rays heat seas, lakes, and damp ground, liquid water becomes water vapor and is absorbed into the air. This process is called evaporation. As warm air rises up into the sky, it cools and condenses to form clouds. Water droplets fall to earth as rain or snow.

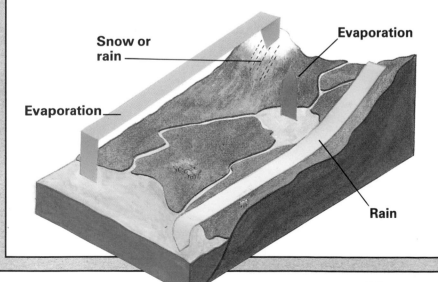

Snow or rain

Evaporation

Evaporation

Rain

CUMULUS
Cumulus clouds are fluffy white heaps that usually indicate fair weather. But they may group together to become rain clouds.

20

CIRRUS

Cirrus are high, wispy clouds which are composed of tiny ice crystals. Winds may blow the crystals into "mares' tails."

CIRROSTRATUS

Cirrostratus clouds form a white veil across the sky. They are made up of thin layers of ice crystals.

CUMULONIMBUS

These are huge, dark storm clouds with flat tops like a blacksmith's anvil. They usually bring rain, hail and thunder – the word nimbus means "rain."

STRATUS

Stratus are low-level blankets of cloud which cover the sky in a dull, gray sheet, bringing rain and drizzle. If stratus clouds rest on the ground or the sea, they are called fog.

FRONTS

Fronts occur where warm air meets cold air. In a cold front, cold air burrows under warm air, causing it to rise rapidly. Clouds, rain and thunderstorms may occur. In a warm front, warm air slides slowly up over cold air, causing rain and drizzle. Symbols for warm and cold fronts appear in black below. When one front catches up with another, an occluded front occurs, causing extensive cloud and rain.

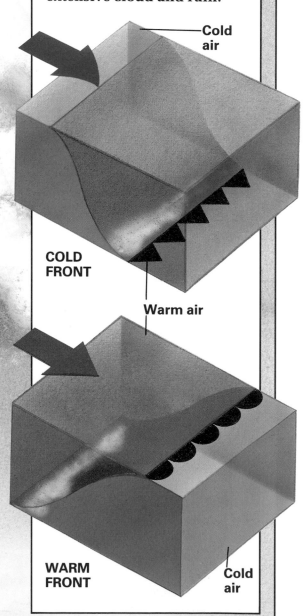

Cold air

COLD FRONT

Warm air

WARM FRONT

Cold air

Try this experiment to see how clouds form. Fill a large plastic bottle to the top with hot water (1). Leave it to stand for several minutes, then pour two-thirds of the water away (2). Stand the bottle in front of a piece of black cardboard (3) and place an ice cube on top of the bottle.

Warm, moist air in the bottle cools as it meets the cold ice cube. Water vapor condenses to form a misty cloud (3).

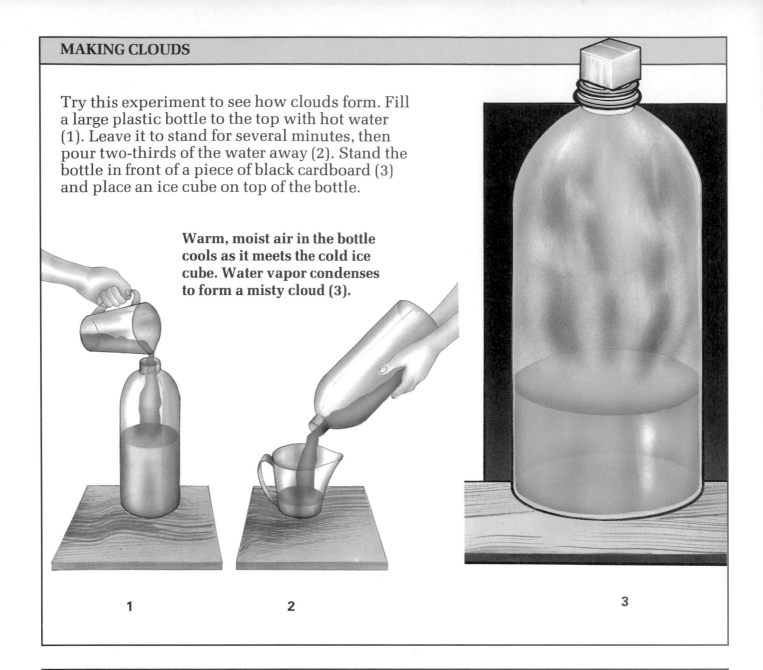

1

2

3

MIST AND FOG

Water vapor in the air sometimes condenses near the ground to form a cloud of water droplets. If we can see less than half a mile through such a cloud, we call it fog. If we can see between one and 1.5 miles, we call it mist. Fog and mist often form at night when cool air causes condensation, and evaporate during the day as the sun warms the air. They also form when warm air meets cold seas or rivers, causing water vapor to condense.

EVAPORATION

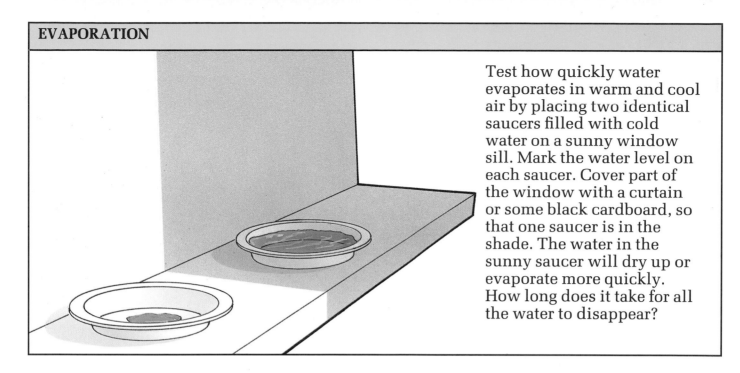

Test how quickly water evaporates in warm and cool air by placing two identical saucers filled with cold water on a sunny window sill. Mark the water level on each saucer. Cover part of the window with a curtain or some black cardboard, so that one saucer is in the shade. The water in the sunny saucer will dry up or evaporate more quickly. How long does it take for all the water to disappear?

MAKING RAIN

Ask an adult to help you with this project. To see how water vapor condenses to form rain, hold a cold spoon in the steam from a kettle. Steam can scald you, so wear an oven mitt and keep your hand well away from the jet of steam. Drops of water form and fall from the spoon, like rain from a cloud.

Oven mitt

Spoon

Droplets of water

WARM AND COOL WATER

As liquids or gases warm up, the particles of which they are made move further apart. This makes them expand and become "lighter," or less dense, and they move upward.

Warm water rises above cold water, just as warm air rises over cool air. Test this yourself with colored ice cubes, made in the ice box with water colored with food dye. Pour warm water into a clear plastic container, and put in a few ice cubes. The cubes will float, but as the ice melts, the cold colored water will sink down to the bottom.

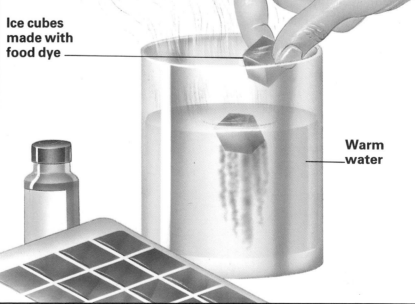

Ice cubes made with food dye

Warm water

SNOW

If the air in a cloud is below freezing, water vapor turns to ice instead of rain. Ice crystals stick to one another to form snowflakes.

HOW MUCH WATER?

Collect snow in a container and mark the level. Measure how much water forms when the snow melts. High on mountains, climbers have to melt large quantities of snow to get enough drinking water.

Each snowflake is unique, but they all have six sides. Look closely at snowflakes with a magnifying glass, and draw some of the patterns you see.

HURRICANES AND TORNADOES

Hurricanes and tornadoes both form in warm, damp air when winds blow into each other from opposite directions. Hurricanes develop over warm, tropical oceans, while tornadoes form over land and are more violent. In a hurricane, the winds swirl around in a spiral at up to 200 mph. In the middle is a calm "eye" 4-25 mi wide, surrounded by the worst wind and driving rain. A tornado is a tall, funnel-shaped whirlwind of cloud up to 2,000 feet high. In the middle is an eye of descending air, surrounded by a strong upward current that sucks up or destroys everything in its path. Tornadoes can travel hundreds of miles before they die down.

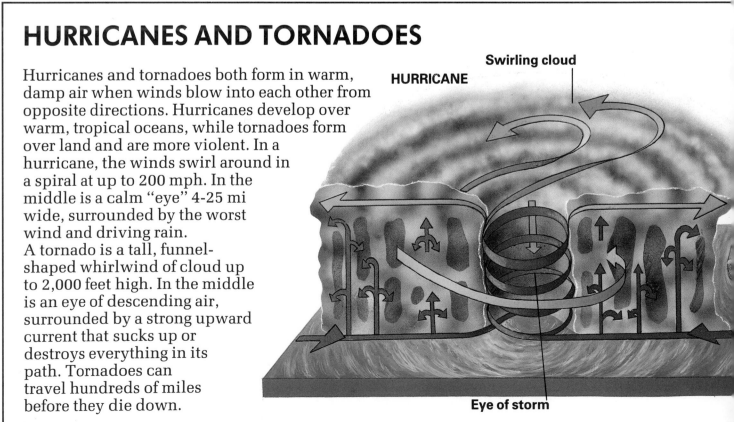

Swirling cloud

HURRICANE

Eye of storm

THUNDER AND LIGHTNING

Thunderstorms occur when warm, moist air rises quickly, forming cumulonimbus clouds. Inside the clouds, fast air currents force droplets of water and ice to rub against each other.

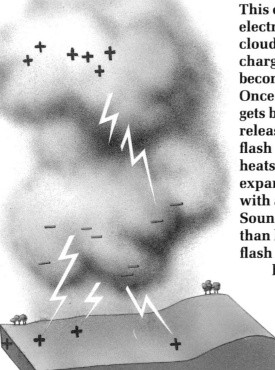

This causes a buildup of static electricity. The top of the cloud becomes positively charged, and the bottom becomes negatively charged. Once the charge at the bottom gets big enough, electricity is released to the ground as a flash of lightning. Lightning heats the air, making it expand quickly and explode with a crash of thunder. Sound travels more slowly than light, so you always see a flash of lightning before you hear the crash of thunder. Lightning takes the quickest path to the ground, often running down tall, isolated objects such as trees.

HAIL

Hail forms when crystals of ice are tossed by winds inside cumulonimbus clouds. As they rise and fall in the cloud, more ice builds up in layers around the crystals: clear ice from the warmer, lower part of the cloud where water freezes slowly, and frosty ice from the colder top, where water freezes instantly.

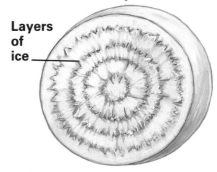

Layers of ice

By cutting a hailstone in half and counting the layers, we can tell how many times it was blown up and down in a cloud.

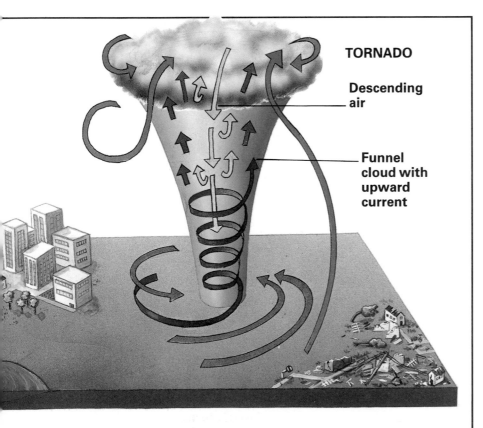

TORNADO

Descending air

Funnel cloud with upward current

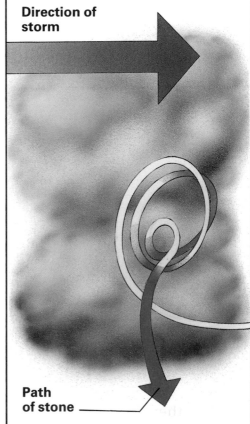

Direction of storm

Path of stone

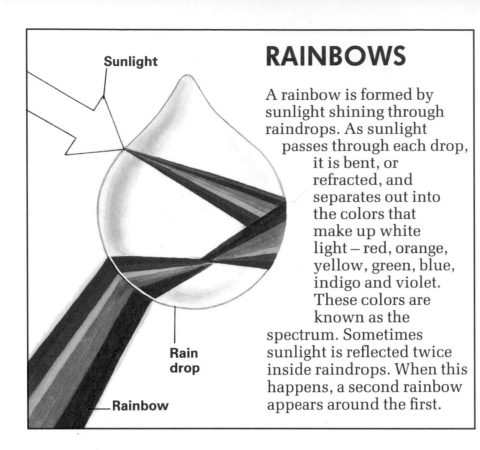

Sunlight

Rain drop

Rainbow

RAINBOWS

A rainbow is formed by sunlight shining through raindrops. As sunlight passes through each drop, it is bent, or refracted, and separates out into the colors that make up white light – red, orange, yellow, green, blue, indigo and violet. These colors are known as the spectrum. Sometimes sunlight is reflected twice inside raindrops. When this happens, a second rainbow appears around the first.

HOW WET IS IT?

Different parts of the earth receive very different amounts of rainfall in a year. Around the equator, the weather is wet all year round. In desert regions, such as the Sahara in Africa, there may be no rain at all for several years. The polar regions also have very little rain because water there is locked up as ice. In India, the land is dry and parched for six months of the year, but soaked by heavy monsoon rains for the rest of the year. In temperate areas, such as Europe, rain may fall throughout the year.

RAIN GAUGE

Weather experts measure rainfall by collecting it in special drums called rain gauges. Rain water is caught in a funnel on top of the drum and runs down into a measuring cylinder.

Make your own rain gauge from a large plastic bottle. Cut off the top of the bottle with scissors (1) and wedge the top upside down in the bottle to form a funnel. Use a ruler to mark a scale in inches on a piece of paper (2) and stick it to the side of the bottle. To prevent the rain gauge from blowing over, you could dig a hole in the ground for it to stand in. Position your rain gauge well away from trees and buildings, where it will not catch extra water dripping down which could distort your records. You could use another measuring cylinder to store a week's rain.

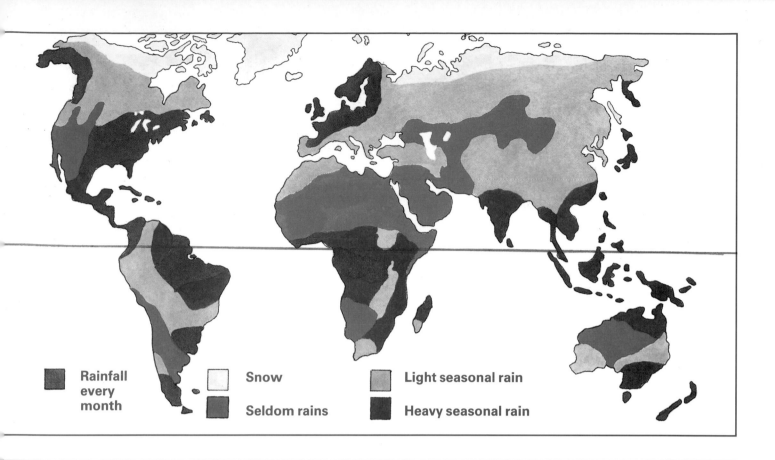

Rainfall every month

Snow

Light seasonal rain

Seldom rains

Heavy seasonal rain

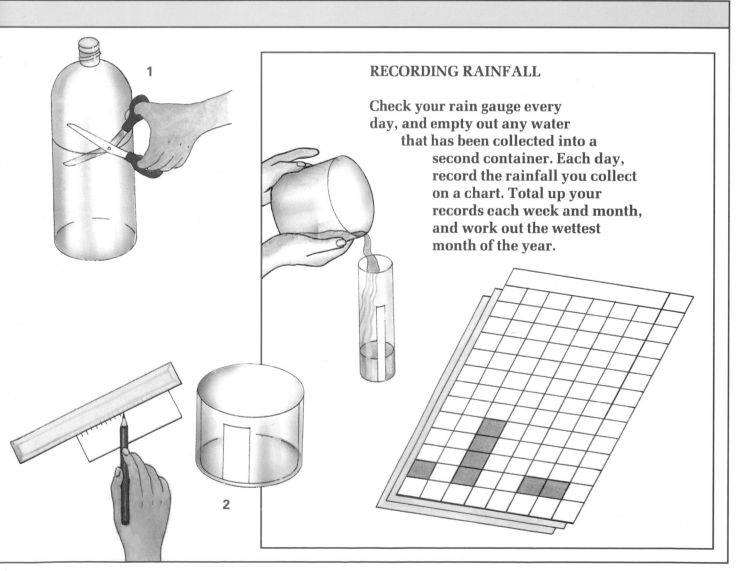

RECORDING RAINFALL

Check your rain gauge every day, and empty out any water that has been collected into a second container. Each day, record the rainfall you collect on a chart. Total up your records each week and month, and work out the wettest month of the year.

1

2

POLLUTION AND CLIMATE CHANGE
THE GREENHOUSE EFFECT

The Greenhouse Effect is a phenomenon caused by gases that exist naturally in the air. These gases allow the sun's rays through the atmosphere to warm the earth, but like the glass in a greenhouse, prevent some of the warmth from returning to space again. As it occurs naturally, this process is essential for life on earth. But if the proportion of "greenhouses gases," particularly carbon dioxide, is increased by pollution, the Greenhouse Effect may be increased, leading to global warming.

If the earth's atmosphere were to warm up even slightly, it might change the weather. Ice caps might melt, resulting in flooding. The main greenhouse gas is carbon dioxide, but methane (from rotting garbage and cattle), nitrous oxides (from fertilizers) and CFCs (from some aerosols and refrigerators) are also important.

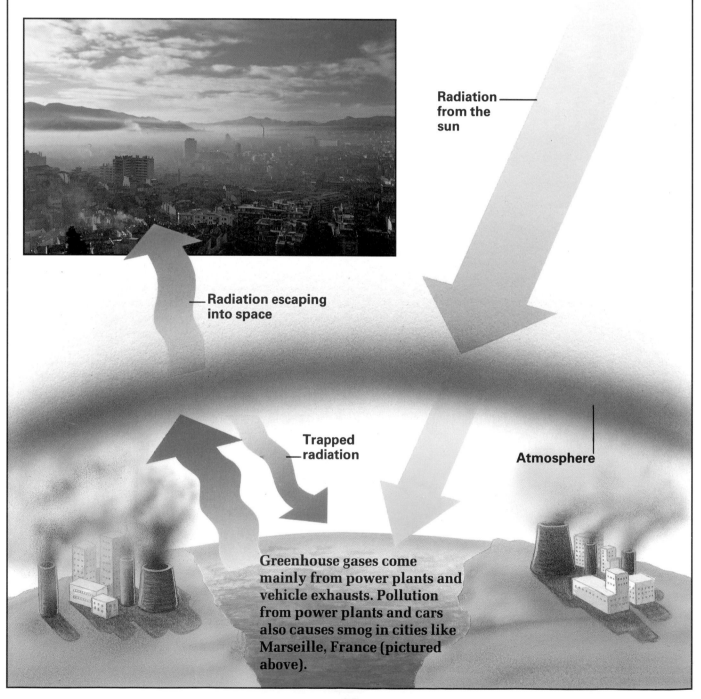

Radiation — from the sun

Radiation escaping into space

Trapped radiation

Atmosphere

Greenhouse gases come mainly from power plants and vehicle exhausts. Pollution from power plants and cars also causes smog in cities like Marseille, France (pictured above).

THE OZONE LAYER

Ozone is a gas which is a form of oxygen. A layer of ozone over 16 miles up in the atmosphere protects the earth from the sun's ultraviolet radiation, which can cause skin cancer and prevent plants from growing. Holes have been discovered in the ozone layer above the Arctic and particularly the Antarctic. Scientists blame gases called chlorofluorocarbons or CFCs, used in some aerosols and refrigerators. Governments have recently agreed to phase out their manufacture.

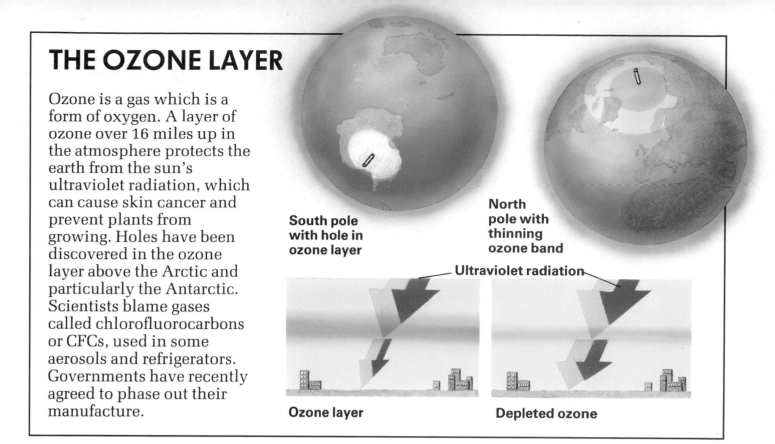

South pole with hole in ozone layer

North pole with thinning ozone band

Ultraviolet radiation

Ozone layer

Depleted ozone

ACID RAIN

Another hazard is acid rain, caused by gases given off by power plants and vehicle exhausts. These pollutants drift in the wind until they come into contact with water in clouds. Then they combine with the water to form sulfuric acid, which falls to the ground with rain. Acid rain eats away at building stone and damages trees, rivers and lakes, killing the creatures that live there.

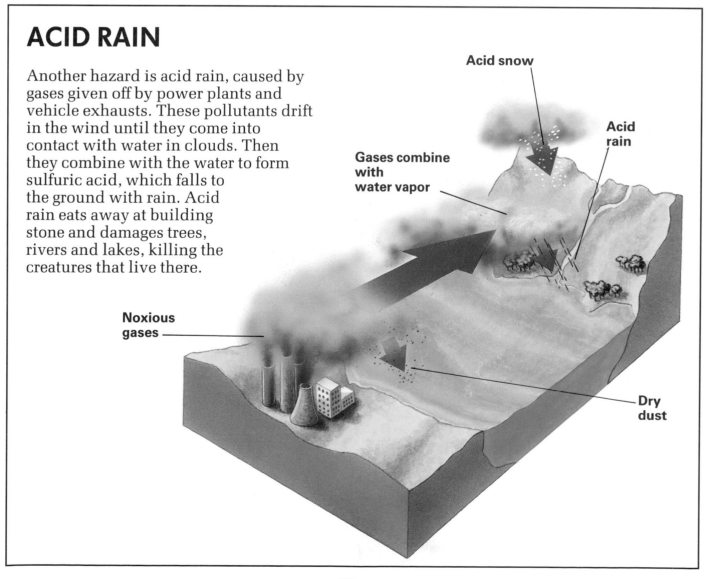

Acid snow

Acid rain

Gases combine with water vapor

Noxious gases

Dry dust

29

MAKING A WEATHER STATION

Weather experts keep their instruments inside a box with slatted sides called a Stevenson Screen. These containers protect the equipment from direct sunlight which could cause false results. The slatted sides allow air to flow freely inside. Your own measurements will be more accurate if you make a container for instruments such as your barometer. Your anemometer could be placed on top.

1. Get an adult to help you cut out the top, bottom and sides of the box from plywood. Make holes in the sides to let air in, and a large hole in the top for your rain gauge.

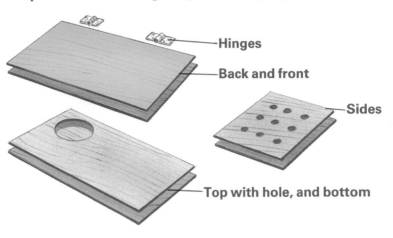

1

Hinges

Back and front

Sides

Top with hole, and bottom

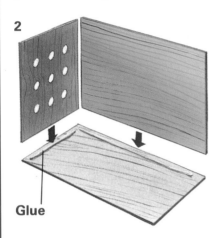

2

Glue

2. Tack or glue the pieces together as shown.

3. Cut four equal lengths of timber for the legs, and screw or nail them to the box. Alternatively, you could stand the box on a table.

3

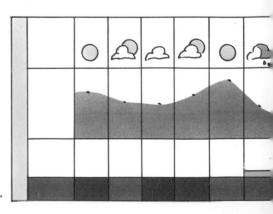

WEATHER CHART

Make a weather chart so you can see the measurements you have made over a month. Invent symbols for different weather features. As you gather more information, it will become easier to predict weather patterns and become an expert weather forecaster.

Graph paper

You could record minimum temperature too.

Color in the wind that prevailed.

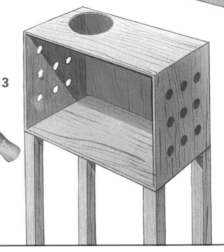

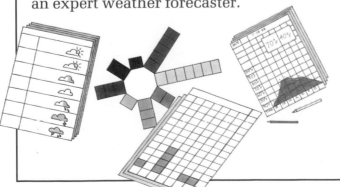

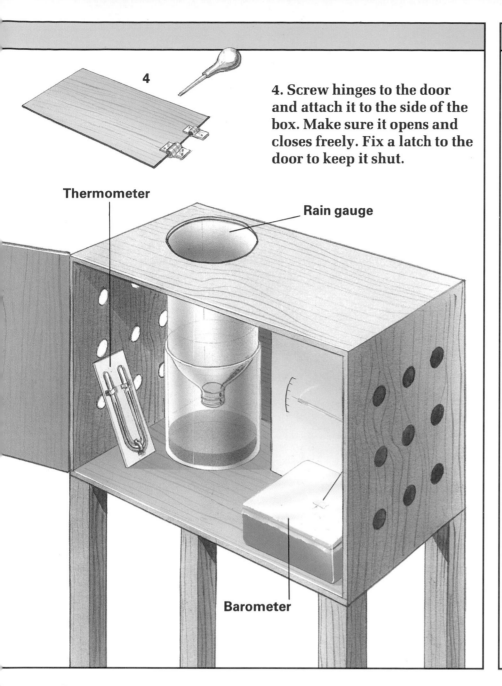

4

4. Screw hinges to the door and attach it to the side of the box. Make sure it opens and closes freely. Fix a latch to the door to keep it shut.

Thermometer

Rain gauge

Barometer

KEEPING A RECORD

To build up a picture of the climate where you live, you will need to record the weather over a period of time. Take your measurements at the same time every day, so that you can compare them easily. Keep records of rainfall, wind speed and direction, temperature, and air pressure. You could also record cloud cover and cloud types. You could file your records on cards in a cardboard box, with dividers to separate different subjects.

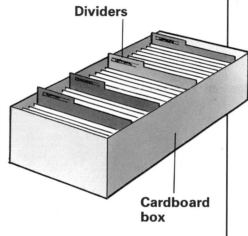

Dividers

Cardboard box

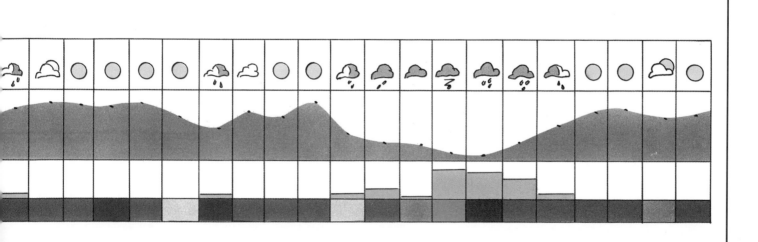

31

GLOSSARY

acid rain rain that is acidic as a result of pollution.

air pressure the weight of the air in the atmosphere pressing down on the earth.

atmosphere the layer of gases (mainly nitrogen and oxygen) that surrounds the earth.

Beaufort Scale the scale devised by Admiral Beaufort for measuring wind speed.

climate the usual pattern of weather in a particular place.

condense to change from a gas or vapor to a liquid, through cooling.

evaporate to change from a liquid to a vapor.

front region where warm air meets cold air. Fronts often tend to bring rain.

global warming the heating of the earth through a buildup of carbon dioxide and other "greenhouse gases" in the atmosphere.

Greenhouse Effect the process by which certain gases in the atmosphere trap heat from the sun, keeping the planet's surface warm enough for life.

hemisphere half a sphere. The equator around the middle of the earth divides the Northern and Southern Hemispheres.

isobar a line on a weather map linking regions where air pressure is the same.

meteorologist scientist who studies information on weather conditions and prepares weather forecasts.

monsoon the rainy season which occurs in India and Southeast Asia.

ozone layer a layer in the atmosphere about 16 mi above the earth's surface, which contains a high concentration of ozone. It prevents harmful ultraviolet radiation from the sun reaching the earth.

Stevenson Screen a box with slatted sides, made to protect weather equipment.

wind a movement of air from one place to another.

INDEX

acid rain 29, 32
air pressure 12-15, 32
air temperature 10, 16
anemometer 18, 19, 30
atmosphere 5, 32

barometers 14, 15, 30
Beaufort Scale 18-19, 32

Celsius 11
climate change 28
clocks 9
clouds 20-22, 26
colors 11, 26
condensation 20, 22, 32
Coriolis effect 16
cyclones 17

days 6, 7
Doldrums 16

evaporation 20, 23, 32

Fahrenheit 11
fog 22
forecasting 14, 15, 30
fronts 21, 32

global warming 28, 32
gravity 14
Greenhouse Effect 28, 32

hail 25
hurricanes 16, 24

insulation 11
isobars 13, 32

lightning 25

maritime climates 8
millibars 12

mist 22
mistral 17

ozone layer 5, 29, 32

pollution 28, 29

rain 14, 15, 20, 21, 23, 24, 26
rain gauge 26, 27
rainbows 26
rainfall 26, 27
Roaring Forties 17

seas 8, 11
seasons 6-9
snow 20, 24
spectrum 26
Stevenson Screen 30, 32
stratosphere 5
sun 4-7, 29
sundials 9

temperature 8, 10-12, 28
thermometers 10
thermosphere 5
thunderstorms 25
tornadoes 24
trade winds 16
troposphere 5
typhoons 17

water cycle 20
water vapor 14, 20, 22-24
weather charts 30
weather maps 13
weather vanes 18
wind 4, 12-13, 16-19, 32
wind rose 19